Flip the Flaps
Dinosaurs

Judy Allen and Tudor Humphries

KINGFISHER

NEW YORK

Contents

KINGFISHER
LONDON & NEW YORK

Copyright © 2008 by Kingfisher
Published in the United States by Kingfisher,
175 Fifth Ave., New York, NY 10010
Kingfisher is an imprint of Macmillan Children's Books, London.
All rights reserved.

Consultant: Michael J. Benton, Department of Earth Sciences, University of Bristol, U.K.

First published in hardback by Kingfisher in 2008
First published in paperback by Kingfisher in 2011
Distributed in the U.S. by Macmillan, 175 Fifth Ave., New York, NY 10010
Distributed in Canada by H.B. Fenn and Company Ltd.,
34 Nixon Road, Bolton, Ontario L7E 1W2

LIBRARY OF CONGRESS CATALOGING-IN-PUBLICATION DATA
Allen, Judy.
  I wonder why flip the flaps dinosaurs / Judy Allen.—1st ed.
    p. cm.
  Includes index.
1. Dinosaurs—Juvenile literature. I. Title.
  QE861.5.A42 2008
  567.9—dc22

ISBN: 978-0-7534-6496-0

Kingfisher books are available for special promotions and premiums. For details contact:
Special Markets Department, Macmillan, 175 Fifth Ave., New York, NY 10010.

For more information, please visit www.kingfisherbooks.com

Printed in China
10 9 8 7 6 5 4 3 2 1
1TR/1210/LFG/UG/157MA

How to say dinosaur names

Allosaurus "al-oh-saw-russ"
Ankylosaurus "an-kie-loh-saw-russ"
Archaeopteryx "ark-ee-opt-er-ix"
Avimimus "ah-vee-meem-us"
Brachiosaurus "brak-ee-oh-saw-russ"
Ceratosaurus "keh-rat-oh-saw-russ"
Compsognathus "komp-sog-nath-us"
Diplodocus "di-plod-oh-kuss"
Dromaeosaur "drom-ee-oh-saw-russ"
Edmontosaurus "ed-mon-toe-saw-russ"
Gallimimus "gal-lee-meem-us"
Iguanodon "ig-wha-noh-don"
Maiasaura "my-ah-saw-rah"
Mamenchisaurus "mah-men-chi-saw-russ"
Parasaurolophus "pa-ra-saw-rol-off-us"
Polacanthus "pol-ah-kan-thus"
Protoceratops "pro-toe-serra-tops"
Psittacosaurus "sit-ak-oh-saw-russ"
Stegoceras "ste-gos-er-as"
Stegosaurus "steg-oh-saw-russ"
Struthiomimus "struth-ee-oh-meem-us"
Triceratops "try-serra-tops"
Tyrannosaurus rex "tie-ran-oh-saw-russ rex"
Velociraptor "vel-oss-ee-rap-tor"

When did the dinosaurs live?

Dinosaurs lived a long time ago—farther back in time than any of us can imagine. They were here before there were any horses or dogs or cats. They were here before there were any people.

Tyrannosaurus rex

1. Did they climb trees to eat leaves?

2. Did dinosaurs eat grass?

3. How did they catch each other to eat?

Velociraptor, a meat eater, pouncing on *Protoceratops*

1. No. Dinosaurs that ate from the treetops had very long necks.

2. No. Grass did not exist when the dinosaurs were alive.

3. Meat eaters hunted other dinosaurs. Some hunted alone, and others hunted in packs. They were very fierce.

Mamenchisaurus eating from a treetop

Fighting back

Plant-eating dinosaurs were hunted by meat eaters, so some of them had body armor. They had horns, spikes, or tails like whips to help fight off attacks. Some lived in big groups in order to protect each other.

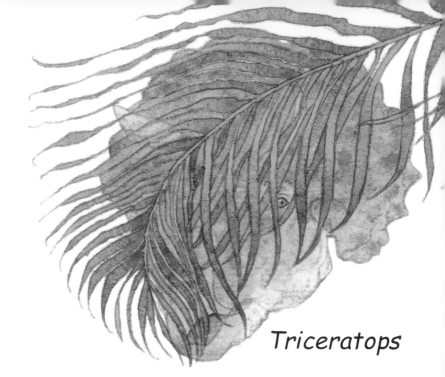

Triceratops

Ceratosaurus

Diplodocus
under attack

1. What kind of armor did *Triceratops* have on its head?

2. Where did *Stegosaurus* have its spikes?

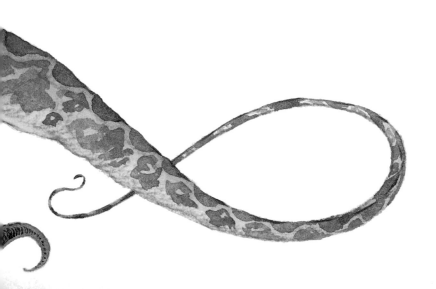

3. Why did *Diplodocus* use its tail as a whip?

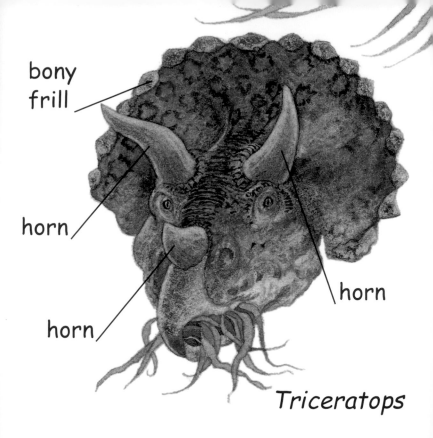

bony frill

horn

horn

horn

Triceratops

1. *Triceratops* had hard and bony frills around its neck. It also had three horns on its head.

2. *Stegosaurus* had four spikes on the end of its tail and some spikes on its back. It could lash out with its spiky tail.

3. *Diplodocus* could use its long tail to whip attackers and knock them down.

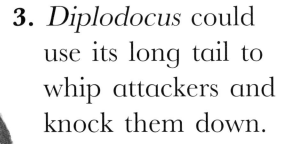

Ceratosaurus
knocked down by tail

Stegosaurus senses danger . . .

turns its back . . .

and swings its tail!

9

Big and small

Dinosaurs came in many different sizes. Some were enormous—much, much bigger than elephants. Some were small—no bigger than chickens—and there were all sizes in between.

Brachiosaurus skeleton in a museum

10

1. What was the
biggest dinosaur?

2. Did dinosaurs
have big teeth?

3. What was the
smallest dinosaur?

1. The biggest plant-eating dinosaur that we know about is *Brachiosaurus*. It was 75 feet (23m) long and 40 feet (12m) high.

2. The meat eaters had big teeth. The plant eaters had small teeth, and the duck-billed dinosaurs had no teeth at all.

3. The smallest dinosaur we know about is *Compsognathus*, which was about the size of a crow.

Compsognathus skeleton

Dinosaur teeth

Allosaurus was a meat eater

big teeth

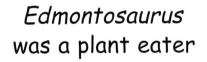
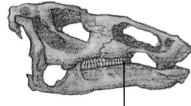

Edmontosaurus was a plant eater

small teeth

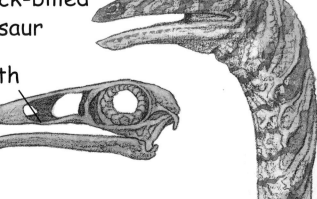

Struthiomimus was a duck-billed dinosaur

no teeth

Babies

Dinosaurs scraped nests out of earth or sand and laid eggs in them. Some covered the eggs in order to hide them and keep them warm. Some sat on their eggs, just like chickens and other birds do today.

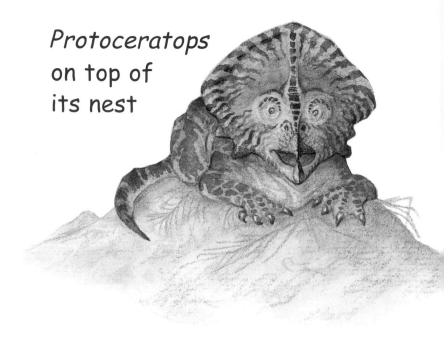

Protoceratops on top of its nest

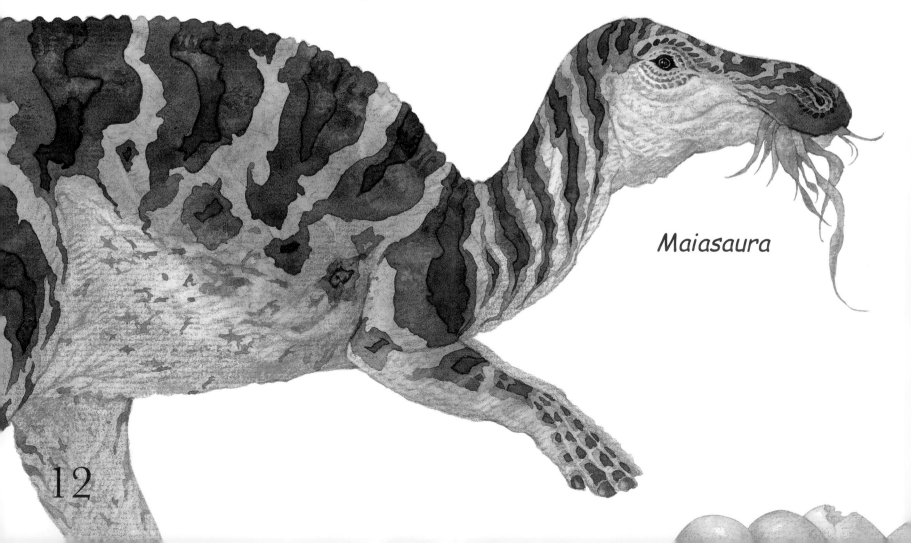

Maiasaura

12

1. Why didn't the eggs break when a dinosaur sat on them?

2. Did the dinosaurs help their babies get out of the eggs?

3. Did dinosaurs feed their babies?

eggs safe in
the nest

Maiasaura
feeding her
babies

1. Only small dinosaurs sat on their eggs. They weren't heavy enough to break them.

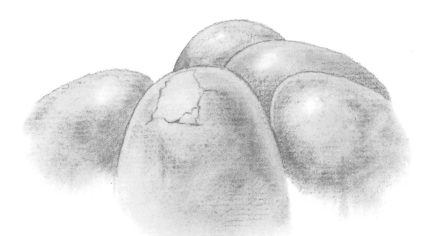

Psittacosaurus egg cracks and . . .

2. No. When they were ready, the babies broke out of the eggs themselves.

a head pops out!

3. Some dinosaurs, like the *Maiasaura*, fed their young. But some dinosaur babies had to find their own food.

The baby then breaks out of the egg.

What happened to the dinosaurs?

A huge asteroid crashed into Earth. There was a great explosion. Dust filled the air so that it was as dark as night. Huge waves and earthquakes shook the land. It was the end of the terrible lizards.

Edmontosaurus grazing

Dromaeosaur

14

1. What is an asteroid?

2. Did the asteroid kill all of the dinosaurs?

3. Are there any dinosaurs left?

asteroid hits
the ground

Dromaeosaur
runs away

1. An asteroid is a piece of rock that travels through space.

2. No, only some. Most of the dinosaurs were killed by earthquakes, drowned by huge waves, and choked by dust.

Avimimus was a dinosaur that looked a little like a bird.

Archaeopteryx was the first bird. It lived with the dinosaurs.

3. Yes. Some dinosaurs changed—over a very long time—into all of the birds that we see today.

Here are some birds that are alive today. 15

How do we know about dinosaurs?

Sometimes, when a dinosaur died, mud covered its body, and over millions of years it turned into a stone fossil. "Fossil" means "dug up," and a lot of fossil dinosaurs have been discovered.

Parasauralophus body lying in wet mud

paleontologists digging for fossils

16

1. What does a fossil
   dinosaur look like?

2. Who digs up
   the dinosaurs?

3. Has anything
   else been found?

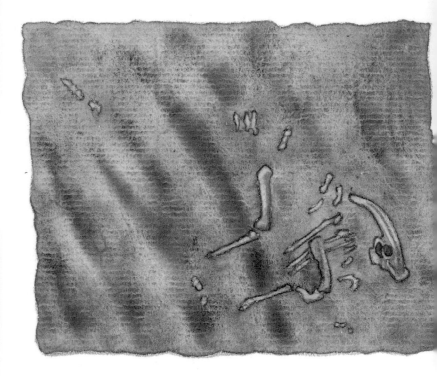

Parasauralophus skeleton
has turned into a fossil

a fossilized dinosaur
skeleton is uncovered

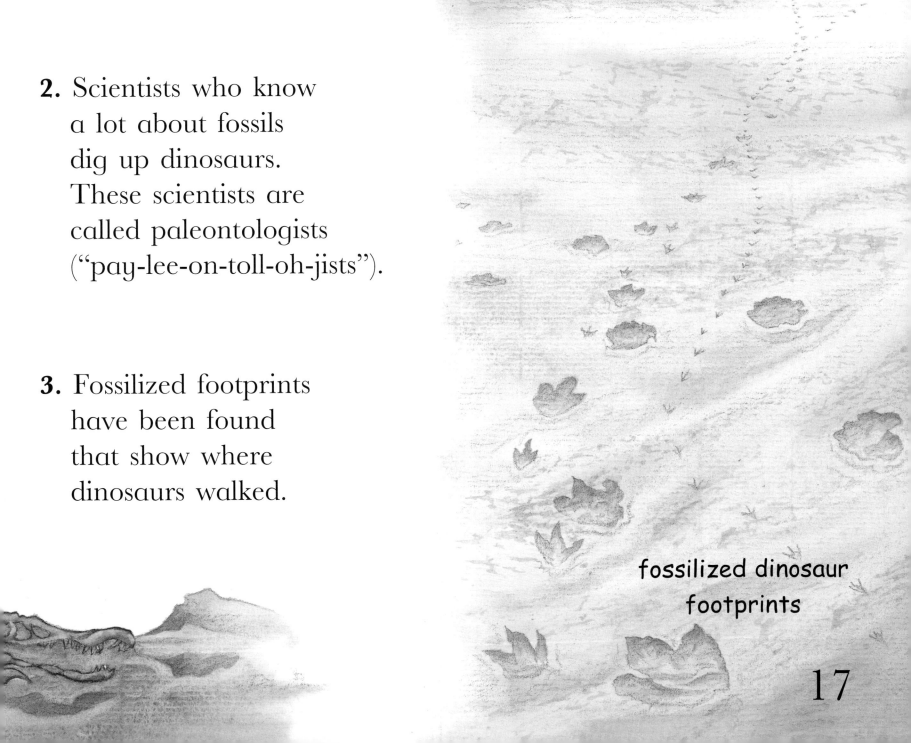

1. A fossil dinosaur looks like a skeleton. Sometimes only part of it is ever found.

2. Scientists who know a lot about fossils dig up dinosaurs. These scientists are called paleontologists ("pay-lee-on-toll-oh-jists").

3. Fossilized footprints have been found that show where dinosaurs walked.

fossilized dinosaur footprints

17

Index

A
asteroids   14, 15

B
babies   12–13
birds   15
body   armor 8

D
duck-billed dinosaurs   11

E
eggs   12, 13

F
food   6–7, 13
footprints   17
fossils   16, 17

H
horns   8, 9

L
legs   5
lizards   5

M
meat eaters   6, 7, 8, 11

N
necks   7
nests   12

P
paleontologists   16, 17
plant eaters   6, 8, 11

S
sizes   10
skeletons   10, 11, 16
spikes   8, 9

T
tails   8, 9
teeth   11